365 WAYS TO SAVE TIME

ALSO FROM LUCY H. HEDRICK

FIVE DAYS TO AN
ORGANIZED LIFE

Lucy H. Hedrick

365
WAYS
TO
SAVE
TIME

Hearst Books
New York

It is the policy of William Morrow and Company, Inc., and its imprints and affiliates, recognizing the importance of preserving what has been written, to print the books we publish on acid-free paper, and we exert our best efforts to that end.

LIBRARY OF CONGRESS CATALOGING-IN-PUBLICATION DATA
Hedrick, Lucy H.
365 ways to save time / Lucy H. Hedrick.
p.   cm.
ISBN 0-688-11751-1
1. Time management.   I. Title.
BF637.T5H43   1992
640'.43—dc20   92-11881
CIP

Printed in the United States of America

First Edition

1   2   3   4   5   6   7   8   9   10

BOOK DESIGN BY KATHRYN PARISE

ACKNOWLEDGMENTS

My heartfelt thanks to Nancy, Toni, Jan, Bonnie, Rick, and Tom, and most especially to Randy Chitwood, Joanne Hoppe, Lucille Kaye, Tom Mullen, Chick Reich, Anne Rockwell, and Barbara Stretton.

INTRODUCTION

There are four organizing tools that I refer to throughout these pages. These tools, if used properly and consistently, will save you a lot of time. They are:

A Pocket Calendar: A calendar whose design you choose—perhaps a-week-at-a-glance or one day per page—which goes everywhere with you.

A Pocket Notebook: A small, preferably loose-leaf notebook where you keep various checklists and that you take everywhere with you. The pages of your notebook are typically titled "Phone Calls," "Errands," "Things to Do," and "Things to

Write," plus any other task or list categories that relate to your life.

(Note: The above two tools are often packaged into "Personal Organizers." There is no right or wrong product. I recommend only that you use the tool(s) that work for you.)

A Tickler File: A group of file folders labeled 1 through 31, one for every day of the month, and twelve additional folders labeled for each month of the year. Your tickler file is where you put papers that you want to have reappear on a specific date. For example, if you send a letter to John Smith on the first of the month and you tell him you'll call him in two weeks, you put your copy of that letter in the "15" file, for fifteenth day of the month. Every day you pull out the file folder for that date, or the month's folder on the first of the month, and take action on its contents.

Permanent Files: A group of file folders for the papers you're saving for future reference (for example, your automobile insurance policy, the warranty for your microwave oven, or the receipts from your credit-card purchases). Your permanent files are stored alphabetically.

365 WAYS TO SAVE TIME

1

Time is a great equalizer. No matter who you are, how much money you have, or where you live on earth, we all have the same twenty-four hours a day. Your time is a valuable resource. Don't waste it.

2

Clutter can slow you down by distracting you from what you want to do. To take control, begin in one corner of one room and straighten it up. (No cheating! Don't just move the clutter to another corner!) Afterward, give yourself a reward for your good work. If you continue this pattern over time, you'll get the job done.

3

Do you often fret over what you haven't done? Don't waste time being anxious about wasting time. Instead, choose one job that needs doing and get moving. Beating up on yourself makes you feel bad and drains your energy. Accomplishing something, and then reinforcing it with a reward, makes you feel better.

4

Do you arrive at your office most mornings frazzled from too much rushing around before leaving the house? Prepare for your departure the night before—put your coat, car keys, and briefcase by the door, ready to grab—and set your alarm fifteen minutes earlier. You'll start your day feeling more in command.

5

If you don't like to forget what you have to do, write it down. Actually, write it down so you *can* forget about it. Now you can concentrate on more important things than remembering.

6

What is the view from your desk? A blank wall? The outdoors? A lot of people passing by? Your view is important. It must be conducive to work rather than being distracting. If your walls are barren, would you benefit from a large photo or print of a garden? Take steps to improve your view today.

7

What is an hour of your time worth? If you earn an annual salary, have you ever figured out your hourly wage? Perhaps you can pay someone else *less* than your rate to do some of the chores you hate. This way you'll have more time to do the work that pays you more.

8

If you spend ten minutes a day looking for things you've misplaced, you waste more than sixty hours a year. Resolve today to put away everything you take out. Also, straighten up one little corner of your world.

9

To feel good and keep stress symptoms at bay, you need to exercise regularly. If you exercise with a friend, you'll be less likely to sabotage your good intentions.

10

Keep a list of rewards in your pocket notebook. When you pass a new shop you'd like to explore, hear of a museum you'd like to visit, or fantasize about having a facial or a massage, write it down. Then the next time you deserve a treat, you'll have oodles of ideas on your rewards list.

11

Do you sometimes feel that you could make better use of little snatches of time? If you knew that you'd be kept waiting for an appointment, that your lunch date would be postponed a half hour, or that your friend who agreed to give you a ride home would be delayed in traffic, would you read a book or magazine, write a thank-you note, plan a menu or guest list? Add some supplies for waiting time to your pocketbook or briefcase.

12

Do you hate to spend time shopping? In your pocket notebook, carry a list of your friends' and loved ones' clothing sizes. When you see the perfect gift idea or a bargain on sale, you can take advantage of your discovery then and there because you're prepared with the information you need.

13

Have you ever worked with a collaborator on a project and felt anxious and frustrated while you waited for the other person to give his or her input and/or pass the project back to you? To avoid the hassles of the waiting game, agree ahead of time on the date of your next discussion or meeting.

14

Do you ever experience "writer's block"? Creative block of any kind is a big time-waster, not to mention an emotional drain. The next time you're stuck, try this unblocking technique: Write a letter to a friend. "Dear John," you might begin, "I have to write a speech for the annual shareholders' meeting and I haven't the vaguest idea of how to start. We've had a lousy year, earnings are down, layoffs are up, but ... let's see ... I guess there are a few bright spots. Two divisions in the south show record profits. . . . " Keep writing to John and your speech will get done.

15

If you have no one to whom you can delegate—indeed, if you're the one to whom everyone else delegates—keep your lines of communication open. Ask your boss or bosses, "What's most important here?" Even if you have too much to do, you will win their favor if you focus on their top priorities.

16

Empty your in basket completely at least once a day. It was not intended for storage.

17

The next time you pass a card store, stock up on a supply of "thank you," "congratulations," and "great job" cards. Keep a supply at the office and some at home. Remember how *you* feel when a good word is sent your way and be generous in your compliments to others.

18

If you've set aside time to do something for yourself, don't be distracted by the dishes in the sink. An illustrator who continues to paint while raising two young sons says that her level of self-esteem at the end of the day is tied directly to her success at focusing on that day's top priority. She has good self-esteem if she paints while her sons nap and if she avoids getting distracted by other things that need doing but are much lower priorities.

19

If you're a pack rat by nature but your possessions are getting out of control, consider this strategy: Establish a "halfway house." Pack up into cartons some clothing, books, papers, etc., that you haven't touched in years. Put a date two years from now on the box and tuck it into a corner. If you don't touch that box before the date, give it the old heave-ho.

20

When someone asks you to help with something you don't have time to do, instead of saying yes right away and regretting it later, say, "I need twenty-four hours to think it over." When you call back to say no, try to suggest someone else who may be able to lend a hand.

21

Are your bookshelves overcrowded? Pass along to friends or loved ones books you have loved but will never read again. Or consider donating a bag of books to one of the annual used-book sales that benefits a school or charity. Some books, however, are like old friends. They should be kept and treasured.

22

If you feel as if you're always rushing, give yourself a chance to unwind with an "R 'n' R" weekend. Look ahead in your calendar and find a weekend that is so far completely uncommitted. Draw a line through it and let that be a visual reminder that you will live serendipitously for two whole days. Wake up Saturday morning and do whatever you feel like doing *for fun* (no chores allowed!).

23

Here's how to plan your day, either first thing in the morning or the evening before: 1. On a clean sheet of paper, write down the appointments that are already written in your pocket calendar. 2. Go to the lists in your pocket notebook and transfer a few important tasks. 3. Add a couple of breaks—fifteen-minute rewards—to provide balance to your day.

24

Do you have a pile of other people's business cards in your top desk drawer? Here's a better strategy to use when someone hands you a card: As soon as you receive it, write on the back where you met this person and what was discussed, and follow up with a call or letter. Then add the information to your Rolodex or mailing list and pitch the card.

25

Do you keep "to do" lists that run on for pages? If you often feel discouraged by what's not crossed off your lists, make them shorter. The most effective managers identify only three top priorities each day. And their self-esteem is stroked repeatedly when they cross off all three tasks, day after day.

26

What do you do with your copy of a letter to which you're waiting for a reply? In other words, where do you put papers that are pending? Instead of keeping them in a "pending" file, "miscellaneous" file, or just a pile, put them in your tickler file where they will reappear on a certain date. When the date arrives and you've had no reply, give a call to follow up. This keeps your plans and your papers moving forward instead of just hanging.

27

Have you ever thought of writing a "not to do" list? This would include any task you can give to someone else, anything done just to please others, and any job whose completion is of little or no consequence. Ask yourself, "What's the worst that could happen if I don't do this?" If the answer is "nothing" or "not much," don't do it.

28

While chatting with a friend or colleague, do you sometimes and think, "Now what was the other thing I wanted to tell him?" If you contact certain people regularly, keep a list titled with that person's name in your pocket notebook. When you think of something you want to bring up, jot it down.

29

Do you feel that you have so much to do, everything seems like an urgent priority and you don't know where to begin? Choose to do work that will bring you immense satisfaction. Weigh one task against the other, and ask yourself, "How will I feel at the end of the day if I accomplish this?"

30

Do you ever try something new—a hobby, sport, or lessons of some kind—but quickly abandon your new endeavor because of lack of time? Before you begin a new hobby or pastime, consider eliminating an old one you've outgrown. Better yet, get rid of two.

31

You'll save money and time used up in shopping if you buy home office supplies in bulk. If you open a charge account, the store will often notify you of special sales and discounts.

32

Filing is a task you can do in your non–peak-energy time. You'll also be more alert and file more quickly if you stand up while working.

33

Decide on a system for storing photographs and their negatives that you'll adhere to from now on.

Most people feel more organized if they put photographs in albums soon after they develop them. Store negatives in envelopes labeled by date and subject and file them in a box chronologically. If you're certain that you're never going to want another copy of Susie on her first day of school, consider throwing the negatives away. They're just more stuff to clutter your life.

34

The most insidious thing about procrastination is that the job grows bigger the longer you keep putting it off. Once started, many people exclaim, "Why, this isn't taking very long at all!"

35

Take time to read a poem. Good poems are lessons in brevity—less is more—and they enrich the soul.

36

When you sort through your mail or your in basket, your first and largest pile should be for the wastebasket (or for recycling). When you perform this action first, you face much less paper to deal with.

37

Shopping by mail-order catalogs can save you time because you can "shop" whenever you like; you're not confined to retail hours. You can look at catalogs while you wait for an appointment, while you commute, or while you take a break from your work. Even though you must pay for shipping, you can often bypass sales tax, depending on which state you live in.

38

Do you ever get so engrossed in what you're doing that you forget to look at your watch? If you work at home, your oven timer can be used to time many things besides your cooking. As an alarm, it can remind you when to leave for an appointment, when to stop what you're doing and start something else, or when to return a phone call. If you work outside the home, a portable timer or a watch with an alarm can fulfill the same purpose.

39

If you don't have time to read your daily newspaper cover to cover, skim the headlines and maybe read the first paragraph of articles that catch your eye. If you have a lengthy report to read for business, rather than feel intimidated by its size and your lack of time, read the first sentence of each paragraph and feel that at least you've made a dent.

40

Are you a chronic clipper of newspaper and magazine articles? Do your files bulge with information you've squirreled away in case you might need it some day? Professional organizers claim that 80 percent of what you file is never retrieved. Instead of clipping, visit your public library, which has, or will tell you where to find, the most up-to-date information.

41

If you were involved in an automobile accident, would you have all the necessary information in your glove compartment—insurance company, policy number, vehicle registration, etc.? No matter which state you live in, a quick call to your local police department will tell you what you're required to carry in your car.

42

Is there anything more discouraging than moving to a new home and realizing you moved many belongings you should have gotten rid of? Plan a house sale of your discarded belongings a month before you move.

43

You can minimize the stress of moving by overlapping your last month in the old location with your first month in the new. It costs you less in time and money to clean up, paint, and make repairs before you move in, provided you can afford the cost of both locations for a month.

44

Keep a file of the sales receipts from having your car serviced, noting the date and the mileage. When you want to sell your car or trade it in, you'll have a tangible service record which may get you a higher price.

45

Do you take enough time to learn from your mistakes? After you make a cold call, have an interview, or deliver a speech, jot down a few notes. First, list everything you did well. Second, note what you would do differently next time. (Do *not* focus on what you did wrong.) Put these notes in your tickler file where you'll find them before your next presentation.

46

In today's world of so-called advanced telecommunications, most people identify "telephone tag" as their biggest time waster. When you leave a phone message on someone's voice mail or answering machine, remember to cover the four Ws: *who* called, *why* you called, *what* you'd like the receiver to do, and *when* you're available to receive a return call. A specific request with detailed information increases your chances of a reply. Furthermore, on the incoming message of *your* answering machine, direct callers to leave you answers to the four Ws.

47

Keep a file of directions to places. When you want to return to a friend's house, meeting place, or country inn, retrieve the directions from your file rather than waste time asking for them again and again.

48

Have you ever thought, while rushing to your departure gate at the airport, "I *know* I've forgotten something"? Before you leave on your much-anticipated vacation, make a list of what you want to bring with you. If you're leaving the country, learn the currency that's accepted, the electrical current for your shaver, hair dryer, etc., and whether you'll need proof of citizenship to return.

49

Your subconscious mind is working all the time, even when you're sleeping. Keep pencil and paper on your bedside table so you can write down that solution to a problem, that twist in your novel's plot, or that bit of family news to tell your daughter away at college when it awakens you.

50

Is yours a recycling home or a recycling office? Save time *and* the environment with clearly labeled receptacles for newspaper, mixed paper, and other recyclables. The containers don't have to be elaborate. Empty cartons will do.

51

Do you often misplace your claim checks for the dry cleaner, photo developing, shoe repair, etc.? Carry them in your wallet. Even if you have a charge account for these services, you probably always have your wallet close at hand when picking up these items.

52

Do you remember hearing the adage "To save time, do two or three things at once?" Times change. The wisdom gleaned from so much frenetic activity—and the resulting burnout and slipshod quality—is now: "Do one thing at a time and do it well."

53

It's important to keep a personal history of the work you do and the skills you learn over time. Set up a "chron," or chronological, file for yourself and your family members. The next time you're asked for your résumé, biography, or background summary, you'll have a ready record from the letters, awards, news clippings, etc., in your chron file.

54

To start yourself off on the right foot each day, read something inspirational every morning. Some of my favorites are poems, page-a-day calendars, and the comic strip *Cathy*.

55

Do you love fresh flowers but hate working in the garden? Or do you plant a garden enthusiastically every spring, only to lose interest before the Fourth of July? Consider investing in some hardy perennial varieties which come up every year. Perennials usually establish themselves quickly, grow more densely, and spread every year. They also require a minimum of fuss.

56

An executive I know says that while he carries a week-at-a-glance pocket calendar wherever he goes, he often needs to look at a whole year. He buys a year-at-a-glance poster, mounts it on his office wall, and plots everything from sales conferences to family vacations, from budget deadlines to his annual physical.

57

How do you remember when it's time to service your car? Maintenance schedules are based on time elapsed as well as mileage driven. Place reminders at appropriate intervals in your tickler file to check your mileage and perform recommended service. You will prolong the life of your car and cut down on costly repairs.

58

In this age of too much information, we often put off making a decision because we feel overwhelmed by all the research we should do. If you don't have enough time to look into what computer to buy, what investments to make, or how to decorate your office, for example, save time and costly mistakes by paying experts for their knowledge. However, to be certain your expert is professional, ask for references.

59

A sure antidote to procrastination is to work with a friend. By collaborating with a congenial partner, whether your goal is to write a book or get fit, to start a business or paint a room, you make yourself accountable to someone else and enjoy creative synergy in the process.

60

Are you the kind of person who always has to be doing something? Experts in human behavior call you a "human doing." In truth, you'll be more productive if, as a "human being," you can sometimes sit quietly and do nothing. Go where your daydreams take you. Take fifteen minutes and just be.

61

A friend of mine confessed that he was afraid to get organized, afraid of the emptiness he would face after he threw away his clutter, filed his important papers, and straightened up his office. I suggested he list half a dozen projects he could tackle after he got organized. Suddenly he realized that there wouldn't be a void, but rather time, space, and clear surfaces to work on.

62

Have you ever left your doctor's office and later recalled questions that you forgot to ask? Prior to your appointment, write a list of your concerns and add to it when another idea pops into your head.

63

When you buy a new appliance, complete your warranty card promptly and keep the owner portion, along with other warranties, in a convenient file. When something breaks down, you can readily locate these papers that explain how to get service or a replacement. A friend of mine adds that he always attaches the sales receipt or, if it was a gift, makes note of the date he received the product.

64

Have you ever vowed to exercise more and then abandoned your good intentions after a short time? Experts say it takes three months for a new habit to take root. After that time, the benefits to you are obvious, sometimes even measurable, and you no longer require so much conscious self-discipline. So if you want exercising to become part of your regular routine, give it at least three months.

65

My friend Lisa's job requires her to travel a great deal. For peace of mind while she's away, she's made a checklist of what precautions to take before she locks her house and departs on her next trip. Her list includes adjusting her thermostat and hot-water heater, putting a few lights on timers, emptying her refrigerator of any perishables, taking out the garbage, and leaving a note for her neighbor who collects her daily newspaper and mail.

66

A CEO I know says that he answers his own phone, takes every call, and insists that his secretary interrupt him when a second call comes in. He argues that this reduces "telephone tag," piles of messages, and time wasted calling someone back.

67

When you're de-trimming your Christmas tree, throw away the tired ornaments you don't want to see again next year, or set them aside and offer them to a nearby thrift shop.

68

Do you ever say to yourself, "I'll get to my big projects after I complete these small, desk-clearing tasks that I can do quickly," and find your day is two-thirds gone by the time you've finished? Resist the temptation to do low-priority work; remove these tasks from your sight. They give you instant gratification in the short term, but take a heavy toll on self-esteem at the end of your day.

69

When you want to paint the interior of your home or office, think "top to bottom." Paint your ceiling first, then the walls, and, finally, take care of your floor treatment. This way you can paint over or clean up any spills.

70

You probably write appointments with other people in your calendar. You can also write down appointments with yourself. When you identify some uncommitted time, choose a task from your "to do" list and make an appointment to do it. This takes you from thinking to doing.

71

There are two reasons why you should group tasks by category (calls, errands, things to do, and things to write) in your pocket notebook: 1. When you sit down to make phone calls, for example, you make several calls and thereby create a sense of momentum. 2. By looking at one list of all the calls you want to make, you're better able to decide which calls are most important and therefore which ones you should place first.

72

Do you complain that you make lists but lose them? Time-management experts recommend keeping all your lists in a small pocket notebook that goes everywhere with you.

73

When someone recommends a book he or she has enjoyed and it sounds like one you'd like, too, write it down in your pocket notebook on a page titled "Books to Read." The next time you're wondering what to bring home from the public library or bookstore, you'll have your list close at hand.

74

A graphic designer who works in a studio at home keeps his work clearly separate from his family life. However, he tells me that practically every room in the house has a wall calendar for quick reference, one or two wastebaskets for recyclables, and a small pad and pencil for jotting down notes.

75

Professional organizers tell us that a "miscellaneous" file can be a dangerous thing. It has a way of growing fat and accumulating many unrelated items. Whatever paper you file, give that folder a specific name.

76

Make yourself an alphabetical index to your files and keep it at the front of your drawer. If you forget where you've put an item, or if you or someone else has to find something in your files, consulting the index will save time in the search.

77

Always have a "Plan B." If something goes awry with your first itinerary, agenda, or schedule, be prepared with a backup plan. You may have to take a different route, but you can still reach your destination.

78

If you have to change your goal—if it's unrealistic or the impediments are too great, or if it's too modest and you know you can do more—realize that goals are only written in pencil, not carved in stone. You may rewrite them at any time.

79

If your travel funds are limited, consider enjoying a weekend away by staying at home. Agree to eat your meals out and visit some of the sights close to home that you've always meant to see. Look ahead in your calendar and plan this kind of weekend today. Your productivity improves when you change your scene and vary your routine.

80

Being neat is not the same as being organized. People who are organized know the next three things they're going to do and the order in which they're going to do them.

81

The paper work for medical insurance claims is often arduous and may be complicated. You can save time and aggravation by setting up file folders at the beginning. You'll need a file for blank claim forms provided by your carrier, a file for duplicates of claims you send to your insurance company along with any correspondence from you or your physician, and a file for the papers from your insurance company when payment is made. Keep bills from doctors in your "bills to be paid" file and move them to your "completed claims" file when all is done.

82

When you make a verbal agreement over the phone, confirm the agreement in a written letter or memo.

83

It has been said that the two-letter word *no* is the single most effective time management tool there is.

84

Are you getting the most from your personal computer? To increase your capabilities and save the time required to research this yourself, consult an expert. Hire him or her for a couple of hours to: 1. tell you what additional things you could be doing; 2. make any adjustments to hardware or install software; and 3. train you in your new enhancements.

85

When you intend to see a first-run movie but then miss it, you know that sooner or later it will come out on video and you can watch it on your VCR. Write the title of the movie on the "Videos to rent" page of your pocket notebook.

86

My friend Tim told me he recently purged the large bulletin board he keeps over his office desk. He threw away everything outdated and no longer relevant. He put business cards into his Rolodex, and entered special events on his calendar. He made note of current discounts or special offers for products on the "Errand" page of his pocket notebook. "All that remains," he says with a laugh, "are take-out menus and inspirational sayings."

87

Separating your professional life from your personal life can be especially difficult when you work at home. Sam, a systems consultant, astounded his family and friends by locking the door to his home office and enjoying a real vacation over the December holidays. During the vacation, if he thought of something business related, he made note in his pocket notebook, but he didn't do any work. Furthermore, he had sent holiday cards to his clients early in December, announcing his vacation dates so that they would know when he was unavailable and when he would return.

88

As someone who was constantly locking myself out of my house and out of my car and then requiring the services of a costly and time-consuming locksmith, I have mended my ways. I carry extra keys at all times.

89

My friend Tom's wallet was stolen. Fortunately, he keeps a list of his credit-card numbers at home and at the office. In addition, his cards are registered with a low-cost consumer protection service. Thanks to this service, he only had to place one telephone call rather than many calls to all the credit-card companies.

90

How well are your investments doing? When was the last time you really looked? If you have interest-bearing CDs, for example, and interest rates are very low, is there another way your money could earn more without sacrificing security? There's never any harm in asking, and if you talk to a banker or a broker, it shouldn't cost you anything.

91

Do you put off filing your income taxes or preparing forms for your accountant because the job
seems so big? Break the job into smaller tasks over
the course of several days—gathering income state-
ments, locating receipts for deductibles and putting
them together by category, and so on—and give
yourself a reward when you complete each step.
For example, you might have a snack, skim the
newspaper, or take a short walk. Plan a big reward
to enjoy when the entire job is done.

92

Gather your gift paper, scissors, ribbon, gift
tags, tape, and shipping supplies in one place and
call it your wrapping center. The next time you
have to wrap or mail a gift, you'll save time by
having all your equipment assembled in one place.

93

Have you loaned items but forgotten to whom? Are you waiting for an answer to a letter or phone call? Keep a list of what's pending or incomplete in your life, cross reference in your tickler file, and cross the item off when it's finished.

94

Pharmacists recommend that you clean out your medicine cabinet once a year. Throw away old prescriptions and over-the-counter medications that have expired. Medicines lose their potency after a certain amount of time. Check the label for the expiration date.

95

Do you have trouble remembering things? Write them down in your pocket notebook. In fact, cultivate the habit of writing things down—a phone call, an errand, a restaurant to try, a vacation resort recommended by a friend, a bright idea.

96

If you have one automobile for business as well as for personal use, it's important to keep track of your business miles, charitable miles, and medical miles which can be deductible on your income tax. Keep a clipboard or small notebook in your car, where you record the date, your destination, the mileage when you depart, and when you return. Tax experts also recommend that you keep track of what you pay for gasoline as well as your other automobile expenses. At the end of the year you'll have this information in one place and you can easily add up your totals.

97

If you have a personal computer and want to minimize the hassle of preparing your tax returns, install a software package that organizes your income and expenses. These programs do all the necessary filing and arithmetic for you. If you spread out your bookkeeping chores and enter your income and expenses as they occur, you'll always have up-to-date totals, and you'll save yourself a big job at year's end.

98

When computers first came on the scene, people thought they would eliminate a lot of the paper in our lives. In fact, just the opposite is true. Do you print a "hard copy" of that letter or memo "just to be safe"? You can save time and space in your files by simply "saving" your work on your hard drive or copying it onto a floppy disk.

99

Karen, the executive director of a nonprofit agency, was determined to purge her files. She could have come into her office over a weekend and put in a dreary day of weeding out the dead wood. Instead, she chose to clean out a half-dozen files each day. At the end of the day, she put six file folders front and center on her desk and then arrived fifteen minutes early in the morning to go through them.

100

As you waited to give your speech, did you ever grimace inwardly as someone did a clumsy job of introducing you? If you want people to know who you are and what you're going to say, be prepared with an introduction that you write and give to the presenter ahead of time. If necessary, include a hint on the correct pronunciation of your name. It saves embarrassment for all concerned.

101

Do you regularly need coins for the Laundromat, parking meter, toll booths, or public transportation? Keep a container handy in your car, at work, or at home, in which you regularly dump change so you'll always have a supply.

102

Have you ever arrived at the theater only to find you left your subscription tickets at home in a desk drawer? Put your tickets in your tickler file for the appropriate date or write a reminder on your daily calendar.

103

Is the personal identification you carry in your wallet accurate and up-to-date? If you were in an accident, would someone know how to contact your next of kin? Would they know your unique medical conditions? Double-check this information today.

104

Several of my friends swear by their tailor-made grocery lists. Each has prepared a list of regularly purchased items and organized it by the aisles of his or her favorite grocery store. Then they duplicated their lists, even having them bound into pads. Now they and all other family members simply leave a check next to various items as they need replenishing.

105

"There's more than one way to skin a cat." There is no one way to be organized. If you have a system that works for you, that's all that matters.

106

Couldn't we all use some comic relief? The next time you hear a decent joke, write it up and give it to a friend. I'm in favor of jokes in the in-basket. Humor adds spice to our lives!

107

How do you store your cleaning supplies? Depending on the size of your living space, consider having a plastic bucket with essential supplies on each floor, under each sink, in each bathroom, and so on.

108

If you take enough time to adapt to a major change in your life—the loss of a loved one, a new job, a new baby—you will experience less stress. Give yourself time to adjust to change. Articulate your feelings in a journal or confide in a friend. Don't rush yourself through this process.

109

Dictating your written correspondence saves time. If you have access to a typing pool, an administrative assistant, or digital voice processing that will transcribe your letters and memos, take advantage of this time-saving asset. You can dictate anytime—before nine, after five, while commuting, etc.—which frees you up to address your more urgent priorities.

110

According to computer experts, it's not a question of whether or not your hard drive will die but rather a question of *when*, and you can bet it will die on a day when you need it. To prevent losing valuable files, you can copy them every day. If you're active on your PC the way I am, however, that could take a lot of time. Save time by purchasing a second removable hard disk. While your system is backing up every day for approximately twenty minutes, do some non-PC work, such as returning phone calls.

111

When was the last time you let yourself just drift slowly through a public library and pick up something that inspired you? If your usual visits to the library are taken up with heavy-duty research, as a reward, allow yourself a vacation in the travel section, the mystery corner, or the film section.

112

Are you tripping over piles of unread magazines but can't bring yourself to part with them? Remember the biblical saying, "There's nothing new under the sun." Every article has been written before and will be written again. So recycle some of those piles. The same articles will be back again in no time!

113

Are you planning to renovate or redecorate the inside of your home? Before you empty your cupboards, closets, drawers, and so on, photograph these spaces with their contents intact so you'll have a record of what you have and how you've stored it. This way, you'll know how to put away your belongings after the paint is dry.

114

Do you hate standing around the baggage claim area at airports, waiting for your luggage? When you travel by air, whenever possible pack a suitcase small enough to be carried on the plane with you.

115

Do you have a reputation for being late? When you keep other people waiting, you send a message that they're not important. Lateness is sometimes the result of unrealistic expectations—you don't allow for possible delays in traffic, inclement weather, or long lines at the checkout counter. Mary, who is always on time, says she always adds thirty minutes to however long she thinks something will take.

116

Not everyone has too much to do. Some people have too much time on their hands, especially people who are retired or out of work. The solution starts with you but involves other people. Pick up the phone and make a date with a friend. If money is tight, suggest chatting over coffee or taking a walk.

117

Family newsletters at holiday time are controversial, according to advice expert Ann Landers, but they save time, prevent writer's cramp, and allow you to stay in touch with many friends.

118

Have you ever said, "I can't clean out the garage today because I don't have garbage bags or cardboard cartons"? A favorite excuse for not starting an organizing project is not having the right equipment. To minimize your excuses, always lay in your supplies before you begin.

119

To some senior-level executives, an "open door policy" symbolizes accessibility. Unfortunately, for others it can mean more distractions and less work accomplished. Don't be afraid to close your office door and leave a friendly note for would-be drop-ins: "Please do not disturb. Income-producing work in progress. Please return for refreshments at 5:30."

120

If you're trying to lose weight, try a positive approach: Instead of writing down everything you eat, record everything you *don't* eat. At the end of a week, you'll feel on top of the world—and lighter on the scale—when you read that you didn't eat bread and butter and dessert at the restaurant, that you said *no* to a second glass of wine at the party, that you pushed away the plate of muffins at the staff meeting.

121

If you're the head of a charity event or fund drive and will be expected to submit a report at the end of the project, keep a little journal in your pocket notebook, or better yet, on your word processor. When it comes time to write your report, you'll already have that record.

122

Why fly far away every time you go on vacation? Some of the best sights to see, hideaways to explore, and retreats to relax in may be within fifty miles of your home. The next time you hear a friend rave about some attraction close by, make a note of it on a page in your pocket notebook. After several recommendations, you'll have a ready-made itinerary for a long weekend.

123

Do you have a supply of press photos of yourself? The first time your employer, civic group, or professional association asks you for a "black and white glossy" head shot, it's time to visit a professional photographer. Order a dozen, size five by seven inches, and ask for more before your supply runs out. F.Y.I.: Your press photos, usually a tax-deductible expense, are throwaways. Don't expect publications to return them.

124

Do you procrastinate on tasks you hate? Everybody does. It's part of the human condition. Get someone else to do what you keep putting off or just let it go.

125

Allen, a marketing executive, has no trouble getting to work on time, but he has a lot of difficulty pushing himself away from his desk at the end of the day and going home. He solved his problem with a little peer pressure. He asked his buddy Ron to walk with him to the train station at the same time every evening.

126

Do you make time for friends? If you complain that no one ever calls you anymore, perhaps you need to be reminded that friendships need fertilizing. In my life, there are friends I pursue, those who pursue me, and those who meet me halfway. I stay in touch with all of them and regularly make plans to get together. It is one of the best uses of my time.

127

Is there a more aggravating question on this earth than "What's for dinner?" To make deciding easier, Julie keeps a loose-leaf notebook where she chronicles her own version of *The 60-Minute Gourmet*. Her pages are divided into menus for company, favorite recipes of her family, and a few pages for new recipes to try. To avoid too-frequent repetition or cries of, "What? Chicken again?" she arranges the recipes in an order she can follow from one day to the next.

128

Meetings don't waste time if the participants are given a deadline and some peer pressure. When participants leave your meetings, they should understand the assignments they must complete before the next gathering.

129

Is a messy desk a sign of a disorganized person? Not necessarily, but a desk littered with personal clutter—old mugs, dried flowers, bent photos, unused paperweights, and so on—usually distracts rather than stimulates your creative juices. If these objects give you comfort, move them to your shelves or credenza.

130

If you want people to pay attention to your speech, don't give them your handout beforehand. Invite them to listen to you without taking notes and then to take with them your brief written summary, available on a table by the door when they leave.

131

Bill travels often on business. To avoid last-minute fretting over what to pack, he carries a travel checklist in his pocket notebook and refers to it every time he starts to pack his suitcase. Actual packing time is kept to a minimum because a set of toiletries, collapsible umbrella, and a travel shaver never leave his suitcase.

132

My friend Susan says that her support group for women going through a divorce actually saves her time. Before she attended meetings, she couldn't get anything done because she was immobilized by her feelings of anger, frustration, and fear. "Now that I get my feelings out," she says, "I can move beyond them, do my job and take care of my children."

133

Have you stopped entertaining because you don't have time to prepare, but you miss seeing your friends? Let go of your mandate to be the perfect host, and invite some friends for potluck. It's exhilarating to watch dinner walk in the door!

134

Car pools to and from work have been shown to increase productivity on the job. Because ride sharers know that their car pool departs from work at the same time each day, they don't waste time during the day and then think, "I can just stay later."

135

Penny operates a successful desktop publishing business from her home. To avoid running out of paper and other office supplies, she places a little reminder on a three-by-five-inch card near the bottom of a supply of, say, yellow paper. Like the notice on top of her last book of bank checks, the three-by-five reminder tells her it's time to reorder.

136

New and old movies aren't the only subjects on videotape. More and more nonfiction and how-to subjects are available at your public library or video rental store. Make a point to check out this area the next time you're pondering what to view. You'll find everything from SAT preparation, to improving your golf swing, to traveling in the United States and abroad.

137

If you send birthday cards to a loved one who lives far away, instead of entering his actual birthday date on your calendar, write "buy and send Bob's birthday card" three or four days ahead of the date. This way you won't become a regular at the "belated birthday" counter.

138

If you could spend an entire day doing something fun for yourself, what would you choose? A day in the country? A day of museums, dinner, and theater? A day curled up in front of a fire surrounded by books or lulled by your all-time film favorites screened on the VCR? Plan a "mental health day" for yourself and resist the temptation to get caught up on chores.

139

Is your desk chair comfortable? Jim, a commercial real-estate broker, was puzzled as to why he avoided working at his desk. Sometimes he spread out in the conference room; at other times he used the desk of an absent colleague. The problem was neither Jim nor his desk, but his chair—it was too low, too hard, and totally uncomfortable. Jim replaced it and worked comfortably ever after.

140

Do you remember the old adage "A place for everything and everything in its place"? When you bring something in, take something off, or set something down, put it in its place right away so you'll always know where to find it.

141

Save time by accumulating your dirty laundry in separate bags or baskets according to washing instructions: warm water, cold water, bleach, etc.

142

Keep a supply of little price tags with strings. The next time you buy or receive as a gift a new suitcase, briefcase, camcorder case, etc., tag those little keys that you usually just throw in a drawer. Two years later when you want to lock your suitcase, you can easily identify the keys.

143

Do you frequently drive long distances in your car? Commuters, traveling salesmen, and even people on vacation have discovered the benefits of listening to audiocassettes. You can learn a foreign language, improve your selling skills, quit smoking, and much more. They're available from your public library, retail bookstore, or by direct mail.

144

As a rule of thumb, store your possessions off the floor. Clutter has a greater tendency to pile up if left on the floor of your closet, basement, attic, garage, and so on.

145

Computers didn't eliminate files from our lives; they added more. Once a year, at a time when you're not at the peak of your energy and yet you want the satisfaction of being productive, delete PC files that are no longer important to you. This way you won't waste space on your hard drive or floppy disks.

146

When you have an unpleasant task to do—ask your boss for a raise, return defective merchandise to a store, reprimand an employee—do it first thing in the morning. Getting the job done and putting it behind you gives your morale a tremendous boost and you'll feel relieved for the rest of the day.

147

As a writer, I have to deal with lengthy book contracts. So much legalese makes me dizzy, but I read them through carefully once and write a brief "we/they" summary. On one side of a piece of paper I note what "we," my agent and I, agree to do, and on the "they" side, I note what the publisher promises. Later on when I want to look up certain details, I can usually find them on my summary page.

148

How do you label your permanent files? Do you write "Car Insurance" and file that alphabetically after "C"? Or do you label your folder "Insurance, Car" and place it after "I"? The point is it doesn't matter. Choose your label so *you* can locate the file and its contents most easily.

149

Are you a "morning person" or a "night person"? Each of us has a biological clock—that is, certain times of day when we are most alert and at peak energy and other times when we're not. You will save time if you do your most difficult or demanding work during your high-energy hours. Postpone your routine chores and low-priority tasks until your "down time."

150

To avoid paying fines for overdue library books, write the due dates in your pocket calendar.

151

If you're afraid of forgetting something you need to take with you in the morning, put it in your car or beside your briefcase the night before. Or post a note to yourself on your bathroom mirror, backdoor, car dashboard, etc.

152

Simplify your schedule. No one can go to every party, every networking event, or every public seminar. Ask yourself if your time wouldn't be better spent one-on-one with a colleague. If your goal in attending is to meet new people, then try to learn ahead of time who and how many will be expected to attend.

153

If you do your ironing and mending yourself, collect these items in one fixed place. You'll waste less time if you set up your ironing board or get out your sewing tools after you've accumulated several pieces to work on.

154

When you pay bills, use your bank's pay-by-phone service, along with your touch-tone telephone. It takes only a few minutes to set up your accounts, and you'll save money in postage, as well as in time.

155

Don't kid yourself that by cutting back on sleep, you can get more done. If you want to do your work well and expeditiously, get enough *zzzzz's*.

156

With creative planning, you can avoid long lines at the post office, bank, or grocery store. Take your lunch hour in the morning or in late afternoon and zip through your errands when there are little or no crowds.

157

Have you ever received the same gift for Christmas from Aunt Margaret in two out of three years? My friend Ann keeps a file labeled "Christmas" in which she puts a list of what she gives her family, one page for every year. So far, no one's received the same pair of socks two years in a row.

158

Do you ever get what I call "term-paper syndrome" just before a deadline and have to "pull an all-nighter" to finish a project on time? You will reduce last-minute stress by using your calendar and spacing the work out over time. If you can, try to give yourself a day or two for extra padding.

159

Do you crave large blocks of time to do creative work, but give in to telephone or people interruptions? Stop feeling like a victim. Ask your secretary to help, use an answering machine, and/or close the door. If you're really distracted, remove yourself to your local branch library.

160

If you're heading up a volunteer effort for your church or office, encouraging others to volunteer— and then getting them to come through for you— is one of life's greatest challenges. You can better guarantee their commitment to work for you (and therefore reduce *your* workload) if they have a sense that all volunteers are pulling an equal weight. List the tasks to be done, then divide them into as many groups as you have volunteers. Write down your plan, including each volunteer's name next to his group. By seeing everyone's assignments written down, no one needs to feel more overburdened than another.

161

Don't run out of your prescription medicines. Place a reminder to reorder in your tickler file or pocket calendar.

162

Do you sometimes feel paralyzed by the number of choices you have? Remember, not deciding is deciding. You can save time and considerable angst by limiting your choices. Commit yourself to visiting only three shoe stores, talking to no more than three building contractors, or comparing just three rental-car rates.

163

If you're prospecting—that is, looking for information, a new job, or the sale of your product or service—you can maximize your time (and theirs) by being prepared. Know something about the person or company to whom you're speaking, have a concise list of questions, and bring a brief brochure or résumé to leave behind.

164

Do you boast that you work best under pressure? It's probably more accurate to say you can *function* under pressure, but in truth, people who work very fast or spread themselves very thin often make mistakes, not to mention increase their stress level. Remember the tortoise and the hare: "Slow and steady wins the race."

165

If you've accumulated debts but now your income is improving, list what you owe and make a specific plan for reducing your liabilities. Otherwise, you might just increase your spending as your income goes up.

166

What kind of appointment calendar or date book do you prefer? There are thousands of varieties on the market, and you should choose the kind that works best for you. To save time, carry your calendar with you at all times and use only that one to write in.

167

Experts in organizing concur that you will accomplish your goals more easily if they are realistic, specific, and measurable. For example, is it *realistic* to double your income in four years, or seven? If you want to improve your marriage, you're being *specific* if you say you're going to arrange "dates" with your spouse for just the two of you two times a month. And if you want to lose weight, you've set a *measurable* goal if you choose to lose five pounds in two weeks.

168

You need to spend time having fun, as well as working, for two reasons: for balance, because "All work and no play makes John a dull boy," and for motivation, because you'll get the job done if you're lured by a fun reward after its completion.

169

Many people complain that they don't have time to plan for the future—they're too busy catching up on yesterday. A friend of mine solved the problem this way: Every year she plans a "personal development day," a whole day spent away from the distractions of work and home, when she contemplates her options for the future. She also identifies people to talk to and other strategies for researching her options. Then, over the months that follow, she chips away at her goals.

170

When you write the name of a person to contact on your to-do list, include the phone number next to his or her name. It's more effective to locate the phone number when you're planning to make the call, rather than when you make the call itself. That way you won't have to waste time looking up the number, when it's time to make the call.

171

Keep a file of all receipts for materials and labor to improve your home. These records may save you taxes when you sell your home.

172

The toll-free 800 telephone number listed on your computer software can save you time. If you don't find the answer quickly in your manual, don't waste time in a futile search. Call the experts.

173

If you're trying to cut back on your spending and live within a budget, don't write down what you spend. Write instead what you *don't* spend. For example, note when you use a discount coupon, when you buy something on sale, and when you resist an item, even when it's on sale.

174

When you're grocery shopping, buy two or more of nonperishable items—canned goods, cleaning supplies, etc. When there's only one left in your cupboard, add the item to your grocery list. Running out of something wastes time because you often have to stop what you're doing to go buy it. It also wastes money because you're more likely to shop at a smaller, more expensive store when you're shopping for only one item.

175

Did you know psychologists say that humans have "nesting instincts" just like birds? Don't fight your urges to organize your clothes closet, straighten your top desk drawer, or make order out of your workbench. It's just Mother Nature at work.

176

Do you know why wine racks position bottles lying down? After many a dry and crumbly cork, I discovered that wine and other corked beverages belong on their side, not standing up. You don't need an expensive wine rack. I store mine on a shelf out of harm's way.

177

When Harriet puts items away at the end of a season—hats and mittens after winter, beach towels after summer, decorations after holidays—she makes sure she doesn't put away what she knows she or her family won't use again. She puts the rejects in a shopping bag and takes them to her thrift shop in hopes that someone else will benefit from them.

178

Don't reinvent the wheel. Before you undertake any new job, find out what's been done before. Talk to people and check your library and other resources.

179

Karen, a busy mother of four teenagers, saves money by buying groceries, including meats, in large quantities. However, between after-school activities and part-time jobs, the teens are all on different schedules, so she freezes meats and casseroles in individual portions, thereby reducing waste from leftovers.

180

George is the dinner-party chef in his family, and to help him get it all on the table hot and on time, he always writes out a schedule of what goes in the oven when. He lists everything he wants to remember, including tasks for the last five minutes before serving time, such as pouring beverages, lighting the candles, etc. This way George can relax and be with his guests in between reminders from his oven timer.

181

To claim a deduction on your income tax for charitable contributions other than cash that total more than five hundred dollars—furniture to the rummage sale, clothes to the thrift shop, a piece of silver to the church auction—the IRS says the value must come from the charity. Since few charities have volunteers enough to assign a value to contributions, you should prepare a list of each item with an appropriate resale price and ask the charity to put its stamp on it. If your noncash contributions come to more than five thousand dollars, there's a different procedure. Check with your accountant.

182

Take advantage of modern technology. If you have a touch-tone telephone and extra services available with it, use the speed calling service. It saves a lot of time.

183

A social life doesn't just happen. You have to plan it. If you live or work alone, you have to give yourself a nudge, pick up the telephone, and make arrangements to see friends. To avoid feeling disappointed and rejected at the last minute, start dialing on Monday to make plans for later in the week or on the weekend.

184

If you want to accomplish a family project—cleaning out the garage, raking leaves, or overhauling the attic—minimize complaining from the troops by starting in the morning, identifying the reward that comes after completion (for example, pizza and a video or a weekday off from chores), and stopping early enough so that everyone has some time for themselves.

185

In these days of environmental awareness, no one should just throw old paint cans, motor oil, and other toxic wastes into the garbage. Put these substances into a carton and keep them out of harm's way until your community plans a toxic-waste day and directs homes and businesses where to take these environmentally harmful substances. Or, call your local sanitation or health department to check on the safest methods of disposal.

186

Rachel's motto is, "Have tape measure, will travel." Her four growing boys are constantly needing bigger sizes. She measures and writes down the pants lengths, sleeve lengths, etc., of their clothes that fit and then shops for bargains on sale. Thanks to her trusty tape, she avoids bringing home the wrong size.

187

Having a good attitude will save you time. We're all dealt many of the same cards in life—job challenges, family disappointments, loss of a loved one—and playing tapes in your head like "I can't,"

"I never will," and "It won't work" will slow you down in your search for solutions. Think positively! It's a big time-saver!

188

If you have a safe-deposit box, do you know what's in it? It's important that someone else—your adult child, a trusted friend, your lawyer—has a list of its contents and knows where to find the key. If you've been thinking about getting a box, do it today. It's the place for stock certificates, the deed to your house, heirloom jewelry, or anything else that would be irreplaceable if lost or stolen from your home.

189

When Barry first moved from the city to the suburbs, he did his errands randomly whenever he needed something. Now that he's made new friends and has better things to do, he saves time by grouping his errands geographically. And since he buys a lot at a discount department store nearby, he keeps a list of items he needs from that store.

190

Do you feel that your life is in a rut? Promise yourself that once a month you will try a new restaurant, get together with a new acquaintance, or visit a place you've never been that's within ten miles of your home. Then tell a friend your intentions and ask him to hold you to it.

191

My friend Bob has a list in his pocket notebook simply called "projects." As an executive recruiter, Bob often has as many as a dozen searches in progress, all at different stages. When he takes ten minutes every morning to plan his day, he looks at that list first and decides what he needs to do to move each search a little closer to completion.

192

Everyone should have days when they don't wake up to an alarm clock in the morning. Let yourself sleep in this weekend, and if your internal alarm clock wakes you up early anyway, play some soft music, prop yourself up against your pillow and read, or just daydream. If you have noisy little kids, trade off sleep-in mornings with your spouse.

193

Going on a diet? Don't just rid your cupboards of fattening temptations; lay in a supply of low-calorie substitutes. When my friend Allen decided to reduce, he drafted a kind of master list of diet groceries—raw vegetables, fruits, popcorn, low-fat diary products, etc.—that he wanted to keep on hand. He said he always took it with him when he shopped so he could retrain his behavior in the grocery store.

194

If you're determined to de-clutter your home, don't say, "This month I'm going to go through my entire house and throw out everything I don't use." You'll be more successful with a more modest goal that's completed on time, such as one drawer, one closet, or one corner in one evening. Then celebrate your success with a small reward and keep up your momentum by setting the next realistic goal.

195

What does it mean when you write lists, but certain tasks just never seem to get crossed off—they continue to stare back at you? It means these tasks were important when you wrote them down, but they're not anymore. Just accept that you're not going to get around to them, and let them go.

196

My friend Ned fancies himself a movie director. Actually, he's the father of four and appears to be permanently attached to his video camera. When he cheers for David's soccer team, he's using the "David tape." When it's Jill's birthday party, he's adding to "Jill's tape." And so on. He tells me he's going to present these "This Is Your Life" tapes to the kids when they're much older. What a great idea!

197

Do you have a "junk drawer" or several of them? If you waste time searching for items you "know are in there somewhere," pick up several of those inexpensive drawer organizers at your hardware or discount store. Or you can use small boxes you come across. It takes a little time to organize the drawer, but you'll save lots more by not having to look for things.

198

Get to be familiar with and comfortable in your local public library. It's amazing how much time and money you can save if you first check the latest information about something. Need a new car, advice about how to work with an architect, or a directory of summer camps? First stop: the library.

199

There's nothing like a little peer pressure to get you moving. Artists I know who paint together, writers who meet and read aloud to each other, and singers who perform for each other say they're motivated to work hard and produce because it would be too embarrassing to show up unprepared or empty-handed. If there's something you want to do, get a bunch of friends together to do it with you.

200

Do you support a few good causes? Make a decision today to "give something back" to people who are less fortunate or to work as a volunteer for something you believe in. Those who do say it's often the best use of their time.

201

If you think you're too busy, too broke, or too fat to have lunch with a friend, it doesn't mean you have to lose touch completely. Calling a friend to chat, even a friend far away, provides a terrific break from your work. Make the call after you adjourn the meeting, hang up the phone with a client, or dot the i's and cross the t's on your final report.

Then the call becomes a reward for accomplishment.

202

Do you love to listen to music but waste time looking for a particular CD, cassette, or album? My friend Tom organized his classical CDs alphabetically by composer. It took a little time to arrange them the first time, but now he can find Brahms with ease—he's right after Beethoven.

203

Do you tend to run out of energy in the afternoon? As an antidote, take a fifteen-to-thirty-minute break from whatever you're doing. If you've been sitting at your desk, take a walk around the block. If you've been outside running from one appointment to another, come in, sit down, and relax. You might also drink some water and eat a piece of fresh fruit. The payoff? You'll return to your work with renewed energy and enthusiasm.

204

Adam has decided that he enjoys organizing his possessions, and therefore, he can turn a chore into entertainment. The arrangement of his neckties is one of his pet amusements. To make deciding what to wear in the morning a little easier (Adam is not a morning person), he has not one, but three, tie racks: one for stripes, one for prints, and one for solids.

205

When I choose a hotel or resort for my vacation, I always ask my travel agent if there's someone from my area who has stayed there. That person can confirm or refute the agent's recommendation of lodging, and also can give me a lot of helpful information about what to expect when I'm there.

206

Recent tragedies involving friends and family losing their homes in a fire moved Bob to videotape the contents of his home. "It's something I had thought about doing for years," he said. "And when I finally made the tape on a Sunday afternoon, I was amazed at how quickly it went." Bob asked his son to help, opening closet doors, drawers, etc., and then he put the tape in his safe-deposit box.

207

Do you have trouble concentrating? Do you turn a forty-five minute task into two hours of drudgery because your thoughts keep wandering and you keep getting distracted? The ability to concentrate is learned, educators say, and it improves with practice. First of all, make sure that if you require total silence, you have it. Second, start out small. Set a goal of thirty minutes of reading the statistical data in that highly technical report. Stop for a ten-minute break before you focus on your reading again.

208

Don't bite off more than you can chew. Learn to say no to extra tasks you don't have the time or energy for. If you say yes and then do the job halfheartedly, the person asking suffers, and so does your self-esteem.

209

Bud is a master at staying off the phone. It's the part of his job that he hates the most; therefore, he delegates 99 percent of it to his secretary. Not only does she answer all of his calls, relay the messages to her boss, and return his replies, she also initiates calls on his behalf. "What would it take to get you to pick up?" I asked Bud. "I guess I'd get on the phone if the President called," he said.

210

"Someday" is not a day of the week. If you want to get something done, commit to a deadline, ask a friend to make you accountable, and then plan your reward.

211

If you're trying to reduce your spending, don't trim your budget so close to the bone that you have no discretionary funds. Pay yourself and your family members a modest "allowance" to spend as each wishes. Your budget will be easier to stick to if you don't feel as if you have to sacrifice everything, including small pleasures.

212

When Marie and Anton flee their high-pressure jobs and head for an island in the sun, they leave behind absolutely everything related to work, including their calendars and pocket notebooks. They each bring lots of books to read, plenty of sunscreen, and a blank spiral notebook "in which I dream," Marie says. "When I relax and wind down on vacation, I daydream about all kinds of things I don't want to forget. I dream about and write down ideas for future vacations, what I might be doing in five years, a guest list for a party . . . whatever."

213

Don't beat a dead horse. When you're trying to think of a solution or trying to get the right idea but it just won't come, relax and give it to your subconscious. Creativity experts tell us that great ideas have to "incubate." Be patient.

214

The first step in tackling any project is to break it down into smaller steps—the individual chores that make up the whole. Brainstorm in pencil, that is, free-associate and write the tasks in any order. Later, edit and order the list.

215

In this era of too much to do in too little time, parents often choose to do at-home chores themselves because they can do them quickly, rather than teach a child to do them, which would take more time at first. But consider the payoffs from delegating chores to kids: They learn a skill, they learn responsibility, and they learn that they have value as members of your family team.

216

You will save time and be more productive if you establish a routine—but one that is flexible, rather than confining, and one that includes time for play as well as work. You can set aside a portion of each day for creative work, for returning phone calls, for meetings, for socializing, for exercising, or for doing nothing. It's your routine; it's your decision.

217

Do you work under proper lighting? Pam was puzzled about why she avoided working at her desk. It was amply large, its surface was free of clutter, and her papers, files, and phone were within reach. Furthermore, she faced a large window with a beautiful view. However, this window, facing east, took in the direct morning sun, which shone right in her face. Proper lighting should be above and slightly behind you. After repositioning her desk, Pam discovered that she loved working there.

218

When you have an appointment with someone, demonstrate that you're not going to waste that person's time. If you're interviewing for a job, making a sales pitch, or just asking for information, make clear up front how much time you need, be prepared with what you're going to say, and take notes on any information, advice, or referrals. By taking notes, you're sending a message that what that person has to say is important.

219

Cultivate the habit of planning your day. Take five to ten minutes every morning or at the end of every evening to plan what work you want to accomplish and what fun you want to have.

220

When you set up your next year's calendar at the end of the current year, you have a terrific opportunity to learn from past situations in which you didn't allow enough time for certain tasks. Want to plan next summer's family vacation, write your department's budget, or start your Christmas shopping a little earlier next year? Choose the ideal time and write it on your calendar.

221

Don't wait for someone to call you in response to your letter. Keep the ball in your court. Always write that you will call during the week of———, and then put your copy of the letter in your tickler file for the appropriate date, or make a note on your calendar.

222

Do you have a well-stocked first-aid kit at home, in your car, or on your boat? Your local Red Cross probably sells them, but if not, be sure yours contains adhesive bandages of several sizes, a triangular bandage in case you have to make a sling, packets of sterilized alcohol swabs for disinfecting a wound, and some antibacterial salve. Check with your doctor or pharmacy for additional suggestions.

223

It's possible sometimes to do two things at once and not sacrifice quality in either endeavor. For example, you can visit with a friend while taking a brisk walk.

224

When you're cooking a recipe that can be frozen, double the recipe and freeze one. For the second meal, rather than duplicate all your effort, all you have to do is set it out to defrost.

225

Do you want to increase your employees' productivity? Form a task force to recommend how to work smarter, not longer. You can motivate them to be more productive by agreeing to share with them the increased earnings that result.

226

Over the past several years, I've noticed that I run out of enthusiasm for Christmas shopping early in December. Many people I know say that they, too, tire of the commercialism and endless buying. Therefore, I make sure to mark deadlines in my calendar so I finish up early. Then I spend the rest of the month concentrating on family traditions, hearing seasonal music, seeing close friends, and reaching out to those less fortunate.

227

Does your job require you to attend large meetings, but your least favorite place on earth is a room full of a hundred people you've never met? One way to minimize your discomfort and increase your chances of making valuable contacts is to arrive early when the crowd is very small. Ask if you can help check people in or write name tags. While you're helping, identify four people whom you'd like to seek out later.

228

Paul, an elected official, says he gets a jump start on his day by arriving at the office thirty minutes before everyone else. He says that this helps him get settled and organized in a relaxed way.

229

Are you bothered by those annoying telemarketing calls that always interrupt you when you're eating dinner? Buy an answering machine, screen your calls, and pick up the phone only when you feel like talking to the caller.

230

Do you need to maintain equipment for your favorite sport—wax your skis, tune your bicycle, sharpen your skates, or scrape and paint the bottom of your boat? Don't get caught unprepared to make full use of the season. Make a note in your calendar to get started well in advance or delegate the maintenance to someone else.

231

Before my neighbor got a new puppy, she went to talk to her local vet. She came prepared with a list of questions including what equipment and puppy food to buy, how often the new puppy should visit the vet, what breed behavior to expect, and a ballpark estimate of the first year's expenses. The veterinarian was very accommodating and didn't charge my neighbor for her appointment, confident that his gift of time had earned him a new customer.

232

Do you spend endless hours shopping for items but not finding what you want in stock? Call ahead and ask before you set out. People who live in cities are masters at saving time in stores. One woman I know telephoned several shops in search of not only the right coat in the right color in the right size, but she also determined the least crowded time to come in and try it on, that the shop didn't charge for alterations, and that they would deliver the coat to her apartment.

233

When you attend an important seminar or conference and learn valuable information, how do you incorporate what you learned into your life? All too often seminar notes get stuck in a file "out of sight, out of mind." During your return travel, or first thing back at the office, go over your notes and highlight actions you want to take. Write them on the appropriate page in your pocket notebook or calendar. If there is information you want to distribute to your staff or colleagues, put it in your tickler file so you remember to do so. Then throw away the rest.

234

If the proliferation of mail-order catalogs is any measure, more and more people don't like (or don't have time) to go shopping. However, shopping can be a reward, as long as you don't bring your list of *everything* the family needs. Go by yourself, at your own pace, and just explore. Who knows? You might stumble on the perfect gift for a friend, a book you've been searching for, or a terrific bargain on sale.

235

Before you move either to a new home or new office, set up a system for letting people know your new address and phone. You can have something printed or use forms available from your local post office. Don't forget to notify magazines, utility companies, and other monthly billers, as well as your clients and friends.

236

Have you ever noticed that when there's a crisis, it's much easier to delegate peripheral tasks? When a loved one is seriously ill or your biggest client is angry and dissatisfied, it's very clear what you have to do, and you can delegate the rest. To improve your delegating skills when there isn't a crisis, imagine that you're in the hospital and you have to ask others for help. This exercise can help you zero in on what work is most important and who in your life is most dependable.

237

Do you know the details of your insurance coverage? Make a note on your calendar to get out your policies a few weeks before they are due for renewal. Consider whether you want to increase your coverage or whether you want to lower your premium by increasing your deductible. Also, for quick reference, write a brief summary of your policy and attach it to the front cover.

238

The next time you need to write a questionnaire or an evaluation, know that more people will cooperate if you provide multiple-choice answers to check rather than if you ask questions that require paragraph answers.

239

Every once in a while, I have what I call a "write-off day," when all my plans go belly-up and I have to let go of all I hoped to accomplish. That's okay. It happens to everyone. You can even have write-off weeks. However, if disastrous days are piling up, you'd better look at the role you might be playing in allowing the crises to happen.

240

A savvy entrepreneur I know did some wise and very effective delegating and some successful marketing in the process: He hired a writer to write his letters. When he read of a client's, or potential client's, promotion in a trade journal, for example, he tore out the page, circled the notice and scribbled, "Tell him congratulations." The writer composed an eloquent letter on business stationery and returned it to the entrepreneur for his signature and mailing.

241

Unless you need some uninspiring bookends, don't keep jars of pennies and other coins. You'll waste money that could be earning you interest in the bank, and you'll waste time when your bank makes *you* put the coins into one-dollar packets in order to deposit them. F.Y.I.: If you carry three quarters, one dime, one nickel, and ten pennies in your pocket at all times, you can make change for any amount under a dollar.

242

If you'd like to eliminate a lot of the junk mail you receive, send your name, address, and phone number to: DMA Mail Preference Service, 11 West 42nd Street, P.O. Box 3861, New York, NY 10163–3861. The Direct Mail Association will take your name off the address lists that they sell.

243

You can reduce your number of trips to the post office if you buy a postal scale and several denominations of stamps. You'll also save time writing mailing labels if you order them printed with your return address.

244

Kitchen cabinets often contain a lot of unused space because the shelves are spaced so far apart. You can increase your storage capacity by adding small, tablelike "step shelves" which you can purchase commercially or make out of wood.

245

Think of six ways you can cut down on repeated errands. Unless it's an emergency, don't take only one item to the dry cleaners. Wait till you have two or more. Likewise, accumulate several reasons to visit the pharmacy, the shoe repair, or the hardware store.

246

Are you hanging on to lots of clothes you don't wear? Have you worn all your suits, your sweaters, or your slacks in the last year? If not, give some away (or give them to your "halfway house"—see #19). Wardrobe consultants suggest that you have at least two or three separates to wear with each piece of clothing. Take your wardrobe "orphans" to the thrift shop where someone else can adopt them.

247

Do you redeem grocery coupons? They save you money on the staples you buy regularly, but be careful that you don't overspend on items you don't need or want. A time-saving way to store coupons is according to the aisles in which your market stocks items.

248

You will save time and money if you take care of your possessions after using them. Clean and store your tools properly, clean the heads of audio- and videocassette players, wipe down your sports equipment when it's gone in the mud, and so on. You'll minimize the cost, frequency and inconvenience of repairs.

249

Do you have a pile of magazines and other "things to read"? My friend used to call hers "Peg's Good Intentions." She complained that when she read two items, the pile then grew by four. When she got through three publications, her pile grew by six. And so on. Now Peg says she reads *smarter*. She first checks the Table of Contents for any articles that interest her. She also has canceled several subscriptions she's no longer interested in. Finally, Peg's new resolution is that if she hasn't read it after four weeks, into the recycling bin it goes.

250

Are there certain times of the year when you routinely experience the blahs? On the last day of Memorial Day weekend when the picnic is over and the parade has passed, do you wish you had something to look forward to? What about after the December holidays, in the doldrums of winter, or in the dog-days of August? Take a moment to think about your seasonal clock and make some plans— they don't have to be elaborate—to lift your spirits.

251

Is it possible you're spending too much on your monthly utility bills? Many fuel, electric, and water companies will visit your home or office at no charge and recommend ways to save energy and reduce costs. Call their customer service office today.

252

Marguerite, a marketing executive, confesses that she practices "selective lateness." Through experience, she knows which clients keep her waiting and which ones don't, and she plans her arrivals accordingly. As a service provider, she can't afford to stomp off in a huff if a client is late, but she's determined to not let it affect *her* productivity.

253

What do you do when you've come to hear a speaker and the program is really boring? If you're not getting what you came for, and if the speaker is not your spouse or best friend, leave. After all, can't you think of something else you'd rather be doing?

254

One hour of concentrated effort is worth more than two hours with interruptions. Each time you're interrupted, it takes time to refocus on the task at hand. Think of three things you can do today to ensure that you have uninterrupted blocks of time. A couple of my personal favorites are a closed door with a DO NOT DISTURB sign and retreating to my local library.

255

When you decide to file a piece of paper, try to file it as soon as you make the decision to do so. If you must postpone your filing, be sure to note on the paper the file folder in which it belongs and, if possible, a date in the future when the paper can be thrown away.

256

When you're writing a letter that asks the receiver to perform an action—for example, to send a donation, register for a conference, or nominate someone for a position—be sure to include a tear-off bill or form on which the reply can be made. Your chances of a response are even greater if you enclose a return envelope.

257

Your calendar is the ideal place to write appointments with yourself to do your gardening chores. From planting and fertilizing to weeding, thinning, and cutting back all the different plants you love to grow, set aside the time for these on your calendar today.

258

Being overstressed wastes time. To keep yourself on a more even keel, eat right, exercise, get enough sleep, and *manage your time*.

259

Is there a cleaning chore you hate? Set up the equipment so you trip over it. Chuck, an artist, hates to vacuum his studio, so he leaves his vacuum out in the middle of the floor at the end of the day. Seeing it there first thing the next morning, he gets the job done quickly—which boosts his morale, as well as his creative juices.

260

If you're moving to a new home, to help the movers, label the rooms and closets in your new home using either names or numbers. Then, as you pack your belongings, label the cartons according to where you want the movers to put them.

261

Credit-card companies and other charge accounts are not infallible. Save your charge slips in a file according to card or store name. Before you pay the bill, check off the charges for which you have receipts and question any charges that are not familiar to you. Then you can throw the slips away (unless the charges are tax-deductible).

262

If you have to do jobs that are downright distasteful to you, consider the time-honored tradition of bartering. When I threw up my hands in despair over a mess with my checking account, a bookkeeper friend came to my rescue. He, in turn, needed help publicizing his services, so I wrote his press releases and marketing letters while he unsnarled my bank account. We both performed the work we know and enjoy, but no money changed hands.

263

When Stan was shopping for a mortgage, he wrote out his questions for the banks, leaving space for the answers, and made several copies. He made his final decision with less hassle because he had organized his research ahead of time. If you're researching something and you're going to be looking at a lot of products or talking to several experts, you, too, can save time if you write up a form for your questions, leaving space for the answers, and make duplicate copies.

264

Help! Your cousins from Omaha just called. They're fifteen minutes away, they're on their way over, and your house is a disaster. To facilitate a quick pick-up, have a "clutter dumpster" in every room. A wicker laundry basket, a large ceramic plant container, or a wooden toy box is just the place to stuff *temporarily* the Sunday paper, the baby's toys, or your pile of mending.

265

What's the best way to learn a new skill: read a book yourself or attend classes with others? Reading a book will probably require less time, provided you stick to it. Taking a class may offer hands-on practice, as well as some peer pressure to study and try your best.

266

People often give you gift ideas in the course of ordinary conversation, or, when you're shopping with a friend or loved one, he or she will give you clues when admiring something on display. Be alert and then jot down what is said in your pocket notebook on a page titled "Gift Ideas for ———." Next Christmas or birthday, surprise friends with the things they really want.

267

People chuckle at the image of an Englishman with his omnipresent umbrella, but Englishmen seldom get wet. Do you keep umbrellas in several locations in case of rain? Don't get caught by inclement weather. Be prepared.

268

If you love books and own a lot of them, design a system so you can find the volume you want when you need it. Consider the approach libraries use: Group nonfiction by subject category and arrange fiction alphabetically by the authors' last names.

269

Many people allege they could be very organized if they could just start over with an empty house, an empty office—in short, an empty life! Alas, we can't wipe the slate clean, but we can learn to strike a balance: a portion of our day spent on current priorities, a portion spent straightening up our backlog, and a portion spent on having fun.

270

An organized office should include two kinds of files: 1. permanent files, arranged alphabetically, where you store information for use later; and 2. a tickler file, arranged chronologically by date, 1 through 31, and by month, January through December, where you store papers and other reminders that you want to reappear on a specific date. Some people also like a file holder on the top of their desk, where they keep current projects.

These are borrowed temporarily from permanent files.

271

As a child, you probably enjoyed collecting things: shells, comics, baseball cards, stuffed animals, and so on. As an adult, you can save time, money, and space if you stop collecting!

272

The least expensive airline rates are more often available if you make your reservations way ahead. If you know you're going to travel, make a note on your calendar to contact your travel agent far in advance to take advantage of the best travel bargains.

273

If you take time to plan, you can do almost all the preparation work for dinner ahead of time. Maryanne works full-time and has three school-age children. She can give her kids more attention when she comes home in the evening by getting a jump start on dinner in the morning. She routinely cuts up salad, marinates meat, and cleans vegetables in the morning. Furthermore, she assigns her kids simple cooking chores to do after school, like putting potatoes in the oven to bake.

274

If you don't have time for a nutritious lunch, you may find yourself yearning for a sweet snack in the afternoon. However, sugar can put a big dent in your productivity. A candy bar, cookies, or rich ice cream will give you a high at first, but in a little while, you'll feel mighty low, even sleepy. When you've got the urge to munch, reach instead for a piece of fruit or whole-grain bread to give your energy a boost.

275

Do you ever feel uncomfortable calling strangers to ask for something—for example, a face-to-face meeting, information, or a reference? You'll save time and reduce your stress level if you get organized ahead of the call. Write yourself a script, including the points you want to make. It doesn't need to be word for word; for some people a three-by-five-inch card with a few mind-jogger notes will suffice.

276

Perfectionism is an enemy of saving time. Do you read something you wrote and revise it, read again, and revise again, ad nauseam? It will never be perfect. Dot your i's and cross your t's, then let it go.

277

What do you do when you're approaching a deadline and you need more time? Panic and accelerate your speed of working and perhaps sacrifice quality? If you suspect you're going to need an extension, let the other party know as early as possible. As long as you don't wait until the last minute, it's very likely you can get more time.

278

Do you have a lot of projects half done? Are your photos half put away in albums, your files half purged, your Christmas cards half written? Focus on one half-done project and spend a little time each day—even just thirty minutes—until it's done. Finishing something adds fuel to your self-esteem.

279

Everyone has become more recycling-conscious. Instead of replacing a product over and over, you will save money, help the environment, and require less storage space by buying refills. The next time you're shopping, check your grocery aisles carefully to see what's new in refills.

280

Have you ever offered the lame excuse, "I wrote it in my calendar, but I forgot to *read* my calendar"? Antidote: Leave your calendar open to tomorrow's date in a place where you'll be sure to see it first thing in the morning.

281

Does your family use portable combination locks? Write down in a safe place the combinations for your bicycle locks, your locker at the fitness center, the cabin of your boat, and so on. If you lose a combination, it's very time-consuming to write away for the numbers and possibly to lose the use of your equipment.

282

If you have a personal computer, it's the best place to keep your address book. If you keep yours on paper, professional organizers suggest a small loose-leaf notebook or a box of three-by-five-inch cards. For a clean, up-to-date look, these have the advantage over commercial books of allowing you to throw away a page or card when someone moves and replacing it with the new address.

283

How do you handle telephone and other messages at home? If you live alone, you get an answering machine—that's easy. If you're part of a family, designate a message center, the first place everyone checks for messages, perhaps even their mail. In addition, pads of pink message slips help children learn to take accurate messages. Finally, make rules for the answering machine—for example, kids may listen to messages but not erase them until a parent arrives home.

284

Many people no longer write personal letters because they say they don't have enough time. However, when I plan some quiet time and write to an old friend, I'm reminded of what a satisfying use of time letter writing is. I can imagine I'm in the same room with her, having a cozy chat, and the miles, as well as the months or years, melt away.

And unlike in a phone call, I get to monopolize the conversation! Write and tell someone you thought of him or her today.

285

If you don't have an answering machine or some-one else to screen your incoming phone calls, learn to do it yourself. If the phone rings while I'm writing and the call isn't important, my stock response is, "I'm conducting an interview." Then I quickly ask what the call is about and when I can call back. If I don't intend to return the call, I say so.

286

You will be more successful in delegating work to others if you make sure you communicate the following: 1. exactly what the task is; 2. why you selected them to do it; 3. the final deadline; 4. checkpoint deadlines; and 5. how you will measure successful completion of the job.

287

In selling, sales managers refer to the "80/20 rule," which says that 80 percent of a salesperson's revenue comes from 20 percent of her clients, that is, from the few customers who place the biggest orders. Similarly, in time management, I believe you get 80 percent of your satisfaction in life from 20 percent, or less, of your time. For example, if taking photographs of nature gives you tremendous satisfaction, it doesn't matter that you sat at a desk all week, as long as you made time to photograph the sunset on the weekend.

288

If you're having trouble getting started on a big job, start with something easy. When my friend Barbara doesn't want to plunge right into a big project, she says she kind of saunters up to it sideways by sitting at her desk and doing some smaller tasks. Sure enough, after twenty or thirty minutes of stretching her muscles, so to speak, she digs right in.

289

If you're going away and leaving your pets in the care of a pet sitter, prepare a list of instructions, including information on pet food, feeding times, and going outdoors, as well as how to contact you and your vet in case of emergency. When you return, *save your list* for the next time you go away.

290

Save time and money by buying in bulk. From pet food to paper products to toiletries, shop every six months and load up. Store the extras away from, but close to, the one that's in use.

291

Can you think of several ways to streamline your actions in a day? For example, Margaret keeps the silverware container to her dishwasher in her sink where she groups together her knives, forks, and spoons so she doesn't have to sort them when she unloads her clean dishes. It's already done.

292

Before you adjourn your meeting, state again the decisions reached and the assignments made. Afterward, send a memo to the participants confirming what took place and the deadlines for everyone's assignments.

293

The old adage about "honey attracting more flies than vinegar" is true. Furthermore, using praise, compliments, and "'atta boys" saves time. When you criticize people, they often pull back and slow down. People will work harder and produce more for you if you stroke them regularly with honest praise.

294

Fear of rejection is an enemy of saving time. We want people to like us, not reject us, and so we continue volunteer commitments and nonessential activities we're no longer excited about. David, a school principal, regained his leisure time by cutting back on volunteer obligations he'd had for years. "We're all dispensable," he told me. "The minute I pulled back, there was someone else to fill my shoes."

295

What do you wish for? Bud says one of his favorite lists in his pocket notebook is his "Wish List." The page includes everything from a CD player for him to a Caribbean vacation for him and his wife to a backyard basketball set for his sons. "It's a list that gets checked off very slowly," he says, "but my wife and I have already booked our vacation."

296

Thanks to today's electronic gadgetry, you can watch quality TV programs whenever you want. Use your VCR to record a program you don't want to miss. Then sit down, relax, and enjoy it as a reward for something you've done. (You deserve it!)

297

You'll save time in making decisions about re-decorating if you determine the focal point of your room. Tom, an interior decorator, explained that a rug, a piece of art, a unique piece of furniture, even a window with a spectacular view, can serve as the focus of your plan. This tip made it easier for me to choose wall colors, fabrics, and floor coverings.

298

Do you ever fall into the trap of rewarding yourself *before* completing a task? For example, do you watch TV to avoid doing something else? Do you chat too long with an office buddy or spend too long on the phone while the budget cries for attention? To stop avoiding and start *doing* takes willpower. However, remember, you don't have to give up "dessert"; you just have to rearrange it!

299

If you live in the snowbelt, are you prepared when the first snow falls? *Before* Ol' Man Winter comes to town, make a note in your calendar to find your snow shovel, sand, de-icer, and other equipment.

300

"Out of sight, out of mind," goes the old saying, and it certainly applies to paper. For example, when a potential customer asks you to call again in six months, don't put that paper "out of sight" in your permanent files. Place it instead in your monthly tickler file, where you know it will resurface at the right time in the future.

301

What do you do when you feel a cold or symptoms of the flu coming on? Do you make adjustments in your schedule and get more rest, or do you go barreling ahead at your usual hectic pace and wind up in bed for a week? You'll reduce your sick time in the long run if you listen to what your body is telling you when you start to sneeze.

302

Do you feel angry when you call a meeting for a certain time but the people arrive late? One way you can communicate to others that your meetings begin on time is to circulate the agenda beforehand and include on the timetable fifteen to twenty minutes before starting time for coffee, chitchat, etc. And then be sure to begin on time.

303

After returning from vacation, have you ever felt overwhelmed by the piles of mail and projects crying for attention? And did you ask yourself if it was worth it to have gone away? Don't lose your vacation perspective! Remember, while winding down you resolved to lighten up. If you can, delegate the sorting of your mail while you're away and begin working an hour earlier the week after you return.

304

Collaboration is a time-saving technique enjoyed by many people in the entertainment field. Consider, for example, the prolific output of Gilbert and Sullivan, Comden and Green, and Rodgers and Hammerstein. After you set a goal, consider getting there with the help of a collaborator. You'll find half the work, twice the fun, and a creative synergy that one person alone cannot achieve.

305

Do you write a to-do list every day, but a big part of Monday's list becomes Tuesday's list which becomes Wednesday's list and so on? Carrying over tasks from one day to the next is a sure sign that your lists are too long. Be realistic. You're probably doing as much as you can.

306

"Maybes" waste time. Try to say yes or no whenever you can and ask others to do the same.

307

Worrying, in my opinion, is the biggest waste of time. To call a halt to worrying, state as clearly as you can what you're worried about. Then ask yourself, "What's the worst that could happen?" Third, identify three things you can do to prevent that possibility. Then take action.

308

If you're having trouble organizing your office, your finances, or your household, hire a professional organizer to help you. When you know you have an appointment with an expert and you're paying for a pro's time, it forces you to identify your problems, to form your questions—in short, to start getting organized.

309

To save time shopping for clothes or gifts, shop by appointment. Many stores, from small boutiques to large department stores, advertise personal shoppers who will help you, one on one, during regular business hours and after hours as well. They can do a lot of legwork ahead of time if you give them your (or another person's) sizes and an idea of what you're looking for.

310

Some insurance carriers will reduce your premiums if you install fire detection equipment such as smoke alarms. They cost very little, are battery operated, and you should own several—near the kitchen, in rooms with fireplaces, and on each level. Fire extinguishers are also recommended. They take a little time to install, but think of how much time it would take to recover from a fire!

311

Buy your Christmas cards, wrapping, ribbons, and so on the day after Christmas when they go on sale for half price. Next fall, buying these holiday essentials will never have to appear on your to-do list.

312

My friend Jan, a writer who enjoys working on several projects at once, distinguishes between ordinary procrastination and what she calls "creative procrastination," or switching back and forth among major goals. She says, "When I stop working on a nonfiction proposal and take up my screenplay again, I'm not putting off the proposal—I'm being creative!" Will switching goals use more time? Probably, but Jan, and many others I know, thrive on variety.

313

Guilt is an enemy of saving time. Don't waste time beating on yourself for what you've done wrong. What's done is done (and hindsight is always 20/20). Remember, it's not your mistakes that count, but what you learn and how you recover from them.

314

For many people, autumn represents a new beginning. Summer's over, school resumes, and the cooler weather gives them new energy. It's a time to examine long-term goals, try on new goals, and plan strategies for achieving them. Whatever time of year you choose, it's important to review periodically what you're doing and where you're going.

315

When I'm traveling, I keep a list of things I forgot to bring. From camping equipment to a piece of clothing to insect repellent, I jot it down in my pocket notebook and then file that paper for future trips.

316

Depending on your stage of life or the time of year, filling up time can be as challenging as finding enough time. Choosing carefully a few activities gives you structure, and a little bit of structure gives shape and purpose to your life.

317

When you receive a letter, try to answer it right away when your thoughts are fresh and your momentum is strong. If you postpone your reply, you'll have to crank up your enthusiasm, as well as remember what to say.

318

Time spent practicing something is time spent well. Whether you're learning to play the piano, rehearsing a speech, or getting used to a new computer program, you need to discipline yourself to practice in order to move from mediocrity to excellence. Remember, the race isn't won by the fastest runners but by those who continue running. Keep practicing.

319

Daydreaming time is quality time. Chuck daydreams while he's fishing, Anne daydreams while she walks her dog, and I daydream while doing aerobics. All of us need to let our minds wander down familiar and unfamiliar paths. In wandering we find the answers to problems, new ideas, and our spiritual selves.

320

Modern technology can save you a lot of time in the kitchen. Even if you love to cook, a microwave oven, a food processor, an automatic coffee maker, and other inventions will give you more free time to do whatever you like.

321

When you're counting down toward a deadline and you can't get an extension for your project, at least try to get rid of everything else. Ask someone else to answer the phone, run the meeting, do the errands, walk the dog—whatever else there is to complicate your life. Until you meet your deadline, do *only* what you have to do.

322

Sometimes you receive an important questionnaire in the mail but you don't want to take time to complete it right away. It's a chore similar to paying bills, so put it in your "bills to be paid" folder and answer the questions the next time you're writing checks.

323

On my personal computer, I have created my own "Help" file. Here's where I write instructions or commands that I use infrequently, but I don't want to waste time looking for them in the manual or calling up my PC-literate friends. Once or twice a year when I need that command, it's only a keystroke away.

324

"Music hath charms to soothe the savage breast," wrote William Congreve in 1697. Modern music lovers recommend this stress-buster: Listen to slow movements by Baroque composers—for example,

Bach, Handel, or Vivaldi. One enterprising friend of mine has made his own audiocassette of soothing sounds. For fans of twentieth-century composers, try Samuel Barber's *Adagio for Strings*.

325

When income tax time comes around, in addition to adding up your income and expenses for the taxable year, you must save proof of what you claim. Keep your income and expense receipts in separate file folders or envelopes according to category— for example, dividend income, charitable deductions, and so on—throughout the year. After you've filed, staple each category together and put them all in one file labeled, for example, "Taxes 1993." The IRS recommends that you save your receipts for at least three years from the date of filing in case you're audited. Most CPA's suggest you save them for ten years.

326

Bonnie, a homemaker and mother of small children, recommends making use of what she calls the "hidden times" in your day when you can grab some time for yourself. With the help of a reliable alarm clock and a caring husband, Bonnie carves out time for herself in early mornings and for a couple of hours on the weekend. "Someone who's a night owl might find some 'hidden time' late at night, after the kids have gone to bed," she adds.

327

Have you ever lost power in a part of your home or apartment and subsequently stared at your electric circuit breaker or fuse box, confused and helpless? You'll save time by making a drawing of the unit, testing each switch, and labeling the drawing. (This is recommended over attaching labels to the switches themselves because tiny labels tend to fall off or become illegible.) And while we're on the subject of power failures, do you know where you keep a couple of reliable flashlights?

328

A time trap that many small-business owners fall into is saying yes to new business when they know they don't have enough time. It's better business not to accept more work than your plate can hold. If you can't do the job, say no, and be confident that from referrals by satisfied customers, there will be more work in the end.

329

Put things where you can reach them easily. It saves time. If you're right-handed, is your phone on your right? Are the kitchen appliances you use most often accessible or must you stand on a step-ladder and rearrange a cupboard to find them?

Sometimes simply a new setup—not a major over-haul—can save a lot of time.

330

Learn to speak and write clearly and concisely. Read a book, take a course, and practice saying it as simply as possible. If someone asks you for a thousand words, don't provide twelve hundred. If you're asked to speak for thirty minutes, don't keep jabbering for forty-five. Too many words waste your time and everyone else's.

331

Keep a list of fifteen-minute rewards, that is, short breaks you can insert into your day that will boost your energy and give a shot to your morale. Your list might include: Take a walk around the block;

skim the sports section of the newspaper; close your eyes and meditate; buy some fresh flowers; play the piano; call a friend to chat; skip stones on a pond; play with your dog; listen to music.

332

Know when to ask for help. You can't always find the answer, solve the problem, or fix what's broken by yourself. Save time by calling an expert.

333

Many people waste time by making small talk up front and then finish by saying what they want. Jim, a man who raises huge sums of money for good causes, says, "You'll save a lot of time if you *begin* by saying what you want from the other person."

334

Do you ever refrain from delegating because it will take too long to teach someone else *how* to do a task? Make the time to train your subordinates. It will pay you many dividends of time in the future. Furthermore, when you invest in training people, you send a message that they're worth it, which in turn, strokes their self-esteem and builds loyalty.

335

Sharon swears by her technique of "office basketry." She sorts her mail and other papers into baskets by priority, the A basket for her most important tasks, B and C for the others. At home, she keeps a portable basket for urgent five-minute tasks such as bills she can pay while waiting for the pasta water to boil, or notices from her children's school that she can read while catching the evening news.

336

Listen, as opposed to hear. Think about the time you waste by asking people to repeat what they said or by thinking you heard them correctly, taking action, and then realizing you misunderstood. Listen *actively* and occasionally take a verbal "snapshot," that is, briefly sum up what's been said. For example, you might say, "Let me see if I understand what you've said so far. . . ."

337

Don't try to put a square peg in a round hole. When looking for a paid job or considering volunteer opportunities, apply your strongest skills to a situation that needs them. If you're a hands-on person, you'll waste your time trying to be a committee volunteer. Similarly, if you prefer the stimulation of lots of people, don't take a job as a solo researcher.

338

When you meet a negative person, find a way to end the conversation and walk away. A negative person is one of the biggest wastes of time!

339

One of the best entertainments available on audiocassettes is a book on tape. Hearing a fiction classic or a current best-seller read to you can make commuting or traveling by car more enjoyable. My friend Sarah has discovered a way to distract herself from an unpleasant task: She wears her Walkman and listens to the latest thriller while she dusts!

340

Don't sweat the small stuff. If you use your time to react to every little crisis and put out every little fire, you'll never accomplish anything—except fire fighting. Choose your battles. Save your energy and time for the ones that really matter.

341

Don't change more than one important thing in your life at a time. If you're changing jobs, don't have a baby. If you're getting divorced, don't relocate right away. If you're moving, don't have surgery. You'll live longer if you take life's stressful moments one at a time.

342

Do you need to consult the owner's manual every time the digital clock on your VCR starts flashing? Do you cook in the dark rather than replace the light in your microwave oven? Take time to learn how to operate your new appliance. Reading the owner's manual in the beginning can save you lots of time later on.

343

When you're concentrating on something and you have to stop for another appointment, an important interruption, or just because it's time to call it quits for the day, write yourself a quick "Next Action" note: Jot down the very next task that needs doing. This way when you return to your project, you won't waste time trying to recall "what's next."

344

"Stop while you're hot," advised Ernest Hemingway. Whenever you can, stop working at a point of accomplishment rather than in the middle of a problem. That way it's much easier to return to the job.

345

Sometimes a face-to-face meeting with someone saves you time. If you need to meet someone in order to make a decision about him—whether to hire him, for example—don't waste time writing letters or making phone calls. Bring him in.

346

When you meet positive, optimistic people, cultivate them. Think of reasons to be around them, to have them on your team. Optimism is contagious, and it definitely saves time.

347

When you receive an invitation or a meeting notice, write it in your pocket calendar and also write the address and phone number of your destination. Then toss the invitation. If you leave for the event in a rush, you won't suddenly realize you left the invitation at home, and if you're delayed, you'll have the phone number at hand.

348

The next time you feel wound up like a top and stressed to the max, try this relaxation technique: Take time to really look at something—the trunk of a tree, a handful of sand, the shapes of clouds. Breathe deeply and slowly and continue focusing on the object. After fifteen to twenty minutes, you'll feel very refreshed.

349

The idea of moonlighting, or working a second job in the evening, has been around for a long time. While not as well known, the idea of *dawnlighting* is familiar to many writers. I know several authors who write before dawn, only to go off to their "real jobs" from nine to five. If there's something you want to do, consider the peace and quiet of early morning.

350

There will always be more to do than you will ever have time for. Work on what's most important—your top priorities—and let the rest go.

351

Know when to cut your losses. When you've given a great deal of effort—to a job, a relationship, a potential customer—for little or no return, it's time to change directions, to put your energies somewhere else. Set a time limit for results and stick to it.

352

Every office should have an *out* basket. I used to put outgoing mail, library books, items to be photocopied, and more on my dining room table. Now I've reduced clutter (and improved the ambience at dinner) with a simple out basket on a shelf by the back door.

353

Do you have trouble making decisions? Indecision wastes a lot of time and there are tricks to make it easier to resolve. First and foremost, limit your choices. It's so much easier and less time-consuming to choose between, say, red and blue, than to choose among red, blue, green, yellow, purple, and brown. Second, list the pros and cons of each choice and choose the one more weighted with pros. And finally, set a time limit and then choose, no matter what.

354

Design your own checklist for the work that you do. If you sell houses, for example, list the steps from first contact with a customer to final sale. If you plan special events, list all the details you need to consider for every event. Or if you publish books, list all the steps from contracting with an author to promoting the final product. Since you probably work on several projects, each at a different stage of development, your master checklist will help you keep track of where you are and what's next.

355

Learn to use the least amount of energy for the biggest result. Professional advertisers will tell you that it's easier to get Mrs. X to buy more of the detergent she already uses than it is to get her to change brands. In other words, it's easier and more efficient to increase something that's already working than to start something new from scratch.

356

If you're giving a speech or a workshop, it's a very good idea to visit the location and see the room beforehand. Check the room size, seating arrangement, anticipated attendance, and your audiovisual requirements. Know the name of the person to contact in case you have questions or need anything.

357

Carry a pocket calculator to save time. Modern technology has made them almost as thin and small as a business card. Calculators come in handy when you're out to dinner with friends and want to divide up the bill, when you want to convert a price in foreign currency into dollars, when you're revising projections in the sales meeting, and so on.

358

Do you waste time looking for your car keys? When you go into the house, put your car keys in the same place every time. A good location is on a nail by the door.

359

Save transportation time and money by booking appointments for several members of your family back-to-back. You and the kids can visit the dentist or eye doctor on the same afternoon. Be sure to take a book to read or some easy "waiting time" chores.

360

Does your pharmacy, dry cleaner, or liquor store deliver? How about your florist, hardware store, or pizza restaurant? You can save time and energy by taking advantage of delivery services.

361

Store seasonal or seldom-used belongings under your beds. I bought a dozen cardboard boxes— three to a bed—where we store hats, scarves, and mittens in summer, or beach towels, swim goggles, and sunscreen in winter, as well as holiday decorations. A picture diagram of the location and contents of each box stays in the night-table drawer.

362

When you're dying to attend a concert or a play and the tickets are sold out, find out if you can attend a rehearsal. Some performing groups—orchestras, choruses, and others—sell tickets to their rehearsals. The tickets are always less expensive than a regular performance, the caliber of entertainment is just as professional, and the interaction between the conductor or director and performers can be fascinating to watch.

363

When I go to bed when I'm tired, I find I wake up too early in the morning. When I force myself to stay up a little later, I sleep soundly and wake on time. You, too, can get more done and get a better night's sleep if you stay up a little later. If reading makes you fall asleep, and you're turned off by TV, try some noncerebral chore like mending, ironing, or wrapping holiday gifts while listening to music.

364

A woman described to me her life-style, which to outsiders was an enviable one with many homes, many interests, and many friends. When I remarked that she seemed adept at juggling many balls, she said, "My life takes up a lot of brain space." What can you do to unclutter your brain space? Try collecting experiences instead of possessions.

365

Don't promise to travel after you retire, build a boat when the children are grown, or write a book when you have the time. Do it now. Quality time doesn't just happen. You have to make it.

INDEX

Numbers following index entries
refer to tip numbers.